Cafe Cultura Speaks!

An Intergenerational Compilation

Cafe Cultura

Cafe Cultura Speaks!

Copyright © 2016 by Cafe Cultura

All rights reserved. No part of this book may be reproduced or transmitted in any form or by any means without written permission of the author.

ISBN 978-0-692-79612-2

To the young people stepping forward to be the change we wish to see in the world…

Foreword

It is with great excitement that Café Cultura publishes this compilation of spoken word, poetry, and lyrics from our partner artists and youth participants in our programs. We hope the finished product will serve as a culturally relevant and engaging resource for our community, and especially our younger sisters and brothers, to find a sense of personal and collective empowerment.

We are releasing this intergenerational compilation after having been recognized as a 2016 IMAGINE 2020 Fund recipient by Denver Arts & Venues and the Denver Commission on Cultural Affairs. The development of this unique experience was inspired by the seven vision elements that make up the foundation of IMAGINE 2020, Denver's cultural plan, and proudly joins the collective effort in furthering arts, culture and creativity throughout Denver. To learn more about IMAGINE 2020 and how to get involved, please visit IMAGINEDENVER2020.org

For those who do not know about our organization: Café Cultura is an award-winning arts, culture, and youth development organization in Denver that promotes unity and healing among Indigenous peoples through creative expression while empowering youth to find their voice, reclaim oral and written traditions, and become leaders in their communities.

Café Cultura has been providing positive, creative, and engaging community spaces for the Denver metropolitan area for more than twelve years. After the passing of respected elder and veteran poet Abelardo "Lalo" Delgado, we accepted responsibility to continue using our oral and written traditions to provide opportunities for creative expression often not offered in schools or in the larger community. Café Cultura also drew inspiration from the movement connecting Indigenous people from throughout the Americas. We use creative expression to unify people representing southern Indigenous nations, known by terms such as "Chicana/o" and "Latina/o," with those Natives of northern nations, referred to as "American Indian" or "Native American."

Café Cultura hosts one of the best open mic venues in the Denver metropolitan area, and the only space focused on family and youth. We also conduct highly engaging and culturally relevant spoken word/poetry workshops for underserved youth throughout Colorado. Café Cultura partners with select organizations and schools to facilitate an intensive workshop series, publish youth poetry, and organize participant showcases. In an effort to develop young leaders within our community, we also coordinate a youth leadership program for Indigenous youth. If you or your organization is interested in collaborating, feel free to contact us.

For more information about our open mic events, workshops, youth leadership program, and other programs:

info@cafecultura.org

720-394-6589

www.cafecultura.org

Table of Contents

Miracle Worker by Franklin Cruz 1

Mom by Franklin Cruz 5

Gracias a la Vida by Franklin Cruz 7

Sorry, Not Sorry by Rosine Mares 10

Mni Wiconi by Matene Strikes First Jerome 13

An Open Letter to Brown Gurls (and a younger me) by Josie Valadez Fraire 14

I Met a Muxer by Josie Valadez-Fraire 20

Love Is My Revolution by Hannabah Blue 24

I Don't Want to be Sick Anymore by Hannabah Blue 28

Back to Black and White by Hannabah Blue 30

I Am Native American by Tywania Holly 35

Walking by Jozer 39

43 by Jozer 43

You Are Not the Father by Jozer 46

Just Get Over It by Nizhonii Mitchell 49

A Friend by reMARKable 51

Hands Up by reMARKable 54

back to the beginning by Tanaya Winder 56

Sonnet MCLXXXI by Tanaya Winder 59

ten little indians by Tanaya Winder 60

Water Is Life by Lucille Left Hand Bull 62

What Is Beautiful? by Alejandro Jimenez 64

When I Think About My Grandma by Alejandro Jimenez 68

The Answer by Simako Marshall 72

It by Diego Florez 75

Scratching the Surface by Diego Florez 76

First, Second, Third, Fourth by Diego Florez 77

Blue Corn Woman by Eden Nicole 78

In Lak Ech by Eden Nicole 80

I Come From the Corn by Eden Nicole 82

Imagine by Celeste Delgado 85

Removing the Chains by Ara Cruz 87

For You by Ara Cruz 90

If Was a Tortilla by Ara Cruz 94

Beautiful Struggle by Fabiola Flores 98

The Real Me by Marilyn Yobech 100

Miracle Worker by Franklin Cruz

I stand straight and proud
when I talk about my father,
the miracle worker.
Mi Apa came from Mexico
with no passport, job, or English.
But like Jesus with water to wine,
he turned sweat into money with just his hands.
He said that in freezing Idaho potato farms,
he would hold a photo of our family
close to his chest,
like a furnace,
to keep him warm.

In America,
the migrant worker is treated like a superhuman.
So they made my father work winters
that could snatch the spirit out the body.
We stayed up waiting for him
only getting frozen pieces of him back.

My father missed most of my
baseball games and my sister's concerts.
And all we got was an exhausted paycheck.
My mother was forced to be both parents
with an icicle for a father.
All while they took advantage of the miracles my father pulled,
lifting mountains out of our path
till his bones were as broken as his English.
They tried to silence him by exploiting him.
But he is a Phoenix from flame,

reborn in my words
because I spit fire
to keep his light burning.

But these companies
dream of people like this,
who leave their homes desperate to fly.
So they take their money,
give them an umbrella,
call it wings,
and push them off a cliff.

My father grew jetpacks on his way down
and carved a little piece of heaven on the way up,
pulling potatoes out of the ground
like he was pulling us up in the world,
twisting till the dirt let go of us,
till we all graduate,
my sisters get their quinceñeras.
Every dollar he earned
was a step forward for this immigrant family:
doctor's visits,
electric bill,
school supplies.
Every bone he cracked
broke a barrier that kept us back.
His back cracked
and I felt safe enough to come out.
His knees broke
and my sister met the first lady.
Feet torn
but we all speak two languages.
He sacrificed his body
building a home in a land
that still believes he is a tool

before a human.

They worked him for every dollar
he was worth.
Every drop of blood was another coin for them.
So they bled him dry,
irrigating their fields with his sangre.
They only saw him as a weight per dollar tool.
So they thinned him out to pay him less.
Now he looks pale,
like American workers' rights,
see-through,
like the lies they tell,
weak,
like their promises,
like the respect they have for my father.

I know where the miracle came from.
It is a hard work migration from Mexico.
It is a dehydration in a blizzard,
whether in a desert or frost.
America keeps my father thirsty,
crying over sacrifices and hopes.
They collect his tears
selling them back
so he could wash down his doubt.
This is why my dad made amigos with tequila.
If they were going to force him to drink anything,
it might as well warm him up in the cold.
But he knew about keeping good company.
So when he left Idaho and the liquor,
he pulled out the memory of us
from his back pocket.
He said that immediately the frost melted to spring
and it started to rain,

so he drank rebirth.
He started again like a baptism,
like God had plans for him and his family,
like someone was watching out for him.
We grew out of the shit storm of his circumstances
and from the fertilized hearth of his tributes,
we sprouted:
four kids,
one grandchild so far.
A defrosted viejo,
brown bear come north looking for warmer weather
to weather this season of cachorritos.
He raised a den of brown babies
till they all made it out of the cave and into the world.
How could I not be proud of my old man.
Look at the man,
un hombre de sangre oso.
He is the miracle worker.
He is mi apa.

Mom by Franklin Cruz

I am my mother's son,
the one who dare not run
from the dreams his mother wished before him
cooked from the recipes and memories of Mama Nico's memories.
My grandmother who taught my mother to put a little piece of heaven into every bite
so she cooks constellations into food,
pulling stars from the backyard garden
the tomate, cebolla, and tomatillo,
Sencillo es cocinar con una sonrisa
It is easy to cook with a smile
when you know your children are filled with the stardust laughter
of licuado, papas y chorizo
all the love mom can fit in
before she shoots across the sky to work.
She goes to her other garden,
pre-school classrooms she waters every day.
She tips the bottleneck of books and letters soak the calendar carpets
The kids splash in the earliest stories or trains to lunar stations.
My mother knows the recipes to make children into stars.
She bloomed out of Raramuri raíces rooting into the ground.
Her Mexicana mariposa leaves branch out into los cielos
until she launched from the crown of our family tree.
And now you soar through my horizon like a comet.
She is mi ama.
She loves us like a meteorite burning the sky
She impacted the earth,
ignited the first oceanic volcano .

She breaks tectonic plates
and moves continents for me.
despite whatever continent, country, ethnicity my mother was
born into.
She comes from a people who were made of Tonantzin
from the cosmos of Aztlan,
one of the deepest magias.
She instilled in me the brujo blood,
El Curandero corazon.
It does not believe in borders,
only bloodlines.
It does not use money,
only magic.
Hace fuego
y da luz a nuevas vidas.
It gives light to new lives
like my sister's,
like our futures,
like our future children.
She is the ancestral genes of the matriarch
la reina,
la Luna,
Venus.
My greatest children memories:
my mother
mi Madre
mi ama.

Gracias a la Vida by Franklin Cruz

I have been looking for men
like you would search for a song:
in a sea shell,
lifting the skeleton to my ear
to pull a melody from the sea salt,
hoping it is the voice of my future husband.
I look for company in coastline arms,
hoping to erode any shameful barnacles of loneliness,
that I will forget any guilt I hold over myself
for being single and young.
I may be able to get married anywhere in America
but does not mean all of my tios and tias will still accept me.
I may have to divorce from them.
My father and I talk into the catacombs of my queer experience.
He does not shove my polygon body down.

He lets it surf the conversation.
He is able to enjoy my company
like he enjoys the oceans,
breathing in the Atlantic of my laughter.
My father tells me that I am
worthy of happiness
and forget what any of his siblings say.
I tell my father being a gay Mexican
is like being a burnt tortilla
that no one will throw away.
They crack their teeth on my backbone,
swallow my spinal fluid
checking if I still think like a Texan.
I hook my arm around my date
but I have not put out enough bait for him to bite,

and I feel like rotten meat.
Mi apa tells me I am sweet because
I can smile like an eagle in-flight,
that I am more free than the average man.
My father speaks to me
like he is a tailwind pushing me forward
every time another guy rejects me.
I go home,
try to forget when I hug my father,
let his gulf coast arms hug me
till the oil spill of self-doubt is washed away.
If I am ever rejected,
he pulls me off desolate islands of self-pity.
He is the main land,
the big piece of home that always makes me feel safe,
a port that I can dock into.
And he just sees me como su hijo,
coming back from another fishing voyage.
My father was raised conservative
but he only conserved the things
that taught me to love despite
the brine of my skin,
the pollution the world tries to toxify me with.
He knows how to keep an ocean clean of trash.
So when I am still swimming the seas
and become a mackerel to a mako shark,
my tiny fish bones bending in their mouths,
he is the tidal waves
that washes over my scaleless body,
taking the shark teeth from my wounds
to make medals of them.
He tells me that he is proud of the
honorable man I have become,
how I walk like I am deeper than the oceans,
open like the blue seas,

El Mar que no conoce la Tierra.
I am free of all the heaviness these land walkers carry,
that I am boundless and powerful,
and can swallow the coast lines with words.
My father loves me
like the oceans love the moon.

Franklin Cruz is a Latino queer poet living in Denver currently in a biology program at Metropolitan State University. The shy kid who learned the power of his own voice, Franklin has performed throughout the country from the Southwest region, coast to coast. An alumni of Minor Disturbance a youth poetry slam team that has won Brave New Voices an international youth competition, Slam Nuba and Mercury Café both adult slam teams and Café Cultura, a grassroots indigenous spoken word artist collective. He has also taught and performed at Universities across Colorado including CU Boulder, UNC, CSU, Denver University, Colorado School of Mines, CU Denver and more. Franklin's poetry reflects on being a first generation child of immigrant parents, being a brown queer child in a heteronormative patriarchy, and recalling the traditional indigenous faith of curanderismo. Franklin's aims to work in social profit sector and is leading to a cross disciplinary STEAM career using poetry as advocacy for social change, scientific education/awareness and personal mental health practices.

Sorry, Not Sorry by Rosine Mares

I am sorry
I am not the person you wanted
me too be.
I know I do not talk or dress
like other girls.
I do not fit
into their assumed image of me.
OH WELL!!!!!
I am not what you expected
or wanted.
So do not just assume
I am like the rest of these girls.
I am unique.
I am powerful.
Some day
I will fall.
But I will gain strength
to build myself back up.
Do not be like everyone else and
assume I am going to be a housewife with five kids
because I will not!!!!
I know my ancestors wanted me to be more.
I control my own destiny!
No one can stand in my way
BUT ME!
So do not sit there and assume
because you are making
an ass out of
YOU!
NOT ME!
I have overcome so many obstacles.
Walk in my shoes

and see my struggles
before you get on your high horse
to assume what my life would be like or what it is.
I try to better myself
EVERY DAY!
But people see
what they want to see.
I am going to be me.
No one will stop me!
It will not be easy
I AM NOT SORRY
for being different,
trying to succeed
and making something out of myself.
I am still learning,
crawling on all fours.
I will walk one day.
Do not be too surprised.
When I take off running
TO GRADUATION DAY!!!
I am not sorry for always having a book in my face
and wanting more.
I do not let my struggles
push me away or stop me.
I grasp them tightly
until I get blisters and sores.
I learn from my struggles and mistakes.
They help build me up more.
"I am sorry"
is just an old excuse
people use when they do not succeed.
I AM NOT SORRY
because I will.

Rosine Mares: I am 16 years old. I am Apache, Cherokee, and Navajo. I am junior at Brady High School. On my spare time, I love to paint and write poetry. I wrote this poem to remind me that I will be the first one in my family to graduate high school on time and to help me reach my dream of going to college. I want to be a Math teacher, specifically a Geometry teacher, because I am good in math and love helping others.

Mni Wiconi by Matene Strikes First Jerome

Unci Maka,
we hear your cries.
We won't stand
for no more oil lies.
Let the sacred Waters
be life.
Standing Rock,
we stand with you tonight.
When the morning sun will rise,
all our Nations will unite.
Mni wiconi,
water is life.

Matene Strikes First Jerome is Turtle Mountain Ojibwe & Dakota. He is 17 years old and a senior at Longview High School. Matene is a peer mentor & advocate for Native youth, speaking at various youth conferences including Escape, Sienna, UNITY, and Bioneers. He has traveled to Nicaragua for a service learning project to build a playground using recycled materials. He has danced and sang powwow since he could barely walk. He is a chicken dancer and loves sharing his culture with others at schools, events, and whenever he can. He plays lacrosse, beads, quills, and is a wonderful big brother to Hawk (14) and Jeanvieve (6). He plans to study Native American Law, medicine, or fire science. Matene has committed to his traditional spiritual ways and has chosen to never use drugs or alcohol.

An Open Letter to Brown Gurls (and a younger me) by Josie Valadez Fraire

There are so many people in your life
that want to *tell* you who you are.
People will work to make you uncomfortable,
feel undeserving of goodness and love.
Know that this comes from places of discomfort
within themselves;
this does not speak volumes about you,
rather about them.
Please,
be kind to yourself.
Do not allow yourself to become your own worst critic.

Your ability to feel the energies of people is a gift.
But you must realize
that not everyone is capable of holding all that you are
in their arms.
You are too much for some.
Those are the people that will not have the privilege
of feeling the softness of your skin and the warmth of your soul.

Dear Brown Gurls,
this comes from the heart,
a message rooted in your very experiences,
meant to guide you to a place where you are able (*not allowed*)
to be all that you are.
Unrestrained.
Authentically.
Unapologetically.

Dear Brown Gurls,

Cafe Cultura

you are
cultivators of love,
sewing roots so deep
they cannot help but fill the stems of your flowers
with purity and divine energy.
B L O O M.
Let the petals of your being extend.
Continue to
TAKE UP SPACE.
Let your petals absorb every drop of The Sun.
Let the warmth kiss your cheek
and fill your soul with radiance.
That radiance becomes you.
Your roots dig deeper than the colonial wounds
carved into your body.
Ask your Mother.
Sit and listen.
She knows of these wounds.
Her wisdom is abundant
and you may wish to dismiss it.
But She knows
of your body,
for it comes from Hers.

Care for your body.
Do not share it with just anyone.
The person who uses it
will also use *you*,
abuse your very conception of self-worth,
if you allow it
and if you don't.

HEAL slowly,
take your time.
Your body is a wonder

that blesses all eyes that receive it,
a body that is sprouted from Maíz,
our santa madre indígena
standing tall despite the conditions,
enduring even the toughest winds,
so sweet to taste but grueling to grow.

Your body is a vessel
from which to spread love in all ways,
always.
You put out too much love
for it to not come back to you.
It will come back to you.
Do not rush it.
Trust your gut when you feel something is not right.
Your youth does not mean you do not know.
You know.

Do not let your generous heart be the stomping ground:
for partners who will not give you what you need
and then shame you for asking for what you know you deserve;
for partners who wish to write their names on your skin,
attempt to "dirty" your image
but do not wish to be *with* you.
Tell those people that you are not theirs
and you never will be.

Dear one,
protect your heart
Sometimes the potential you see in someone
is not what they allow themselves to achieve.
Although they are from God,
they may not be all that you prayed for.
Rather,

they are a lesson
to help you find love in the arms that are able to envelop all
that you are.

Learn to let go
of the people who try to dull your shine.
Say goodbye:
to all those who do not wish to know you;
to all those who do not *cherish* you;
to all those who pluck your petals,
one by one;
to all those who cut down your stems with dull knives,
getting pleasure from watching your flesh tear;
to all those who don't see that you are the very Wonder of the
World.

Let go of people
without feeling like you are required to give explanations.
Do not feel
like you must explain
why you let them stay
or why you didn't leave.

Young Brown Gurl,
greñuda
unpolished:
May your rawness continue to create discomfort
in the hearts of the complacent.
Make your presence known.
Make them speak your name with the same curiosity
with which they view you.
Never fear being watched by curious eyes
because they are silently taking notes,
wanting to be all that you are,
yet falling short because they do not understand

that you. cannot. be. grasped. so easily.
You are not a soul that floats waiting to captured.
You fly above,
watching over the earth,
Angel de mi guardia.

Your tongue is tough,
leathery like the skin of our campesinos baking in the sun.
Let it loose.
Spit the truth with anger and fury.
Continue speaking your truths,
those of our people,
because they are not always there to do it for themselves.
You may be on a journey that makes you feel alone.

But You. Never. Are.
Make sure to ask for help when you need it.
Cry. Cry often. Cry UGLY.
Take good care of your mind and soul.

Believe, know, and say
that
you are not the exception.
Our people are,
as are you,

People of

Mexcellence

You are a
#sCHOLAr.
Intellect that cannot be measured by a scantron and 175 minutes of time wasted
filling in bubbles,

like the one in which you are forced to live

You are visible.
Dear Brown Gurl,
People watch you.
Let them take notes,
wanting to be all that you are.
But know,
Dear Brown Gurl,
that they
simply
cannot grasp all that you are
and they never will.

With Love and Light,

A Brown Muxer

I Met a Muxer by Josie Valadez-Fraire

I met a muxer:
Divina
Guererra
Strong
like the smell of burning sage and copal
Powerful
Cleansing
Unforgettable

She is
more gorgeous than
the standards She is bound by
"Her beauty could not be measured
by standards of a colonized mind."

Skin rich, brown, gritty, thick
Fertile like the soil from which She sprouted

She is not for everyone.
Some will never feel the warmth of Her skin,
of Her touch.

She is not easy to swallow
for Her edges cut the throats
of men,
their skin too fragile to contain Her sharpness,
unable to hold Her abundance in their small minds and arms.
Men
are fragile,
it seems
too fragile
for Her presence.

But She,
She is gentle.
She releases energy that brings them back
to life
The wounds caused by Her grit
are shallow compared to Her depth.

Her wounds deep,
Heart
Not broken
but healing
Tender
like Her
Wounds
begging to be healed
Curandera
BRUJA
healer of dormant hearts
Spiritual Goddess
Diosa.

The weak cower in Her presence.
She was rough,
unpolished,
a diamond waiting to become
Always becoming
I saw Her glow
illuminating the darkest spaces
within my heart.
She too is darkness.
Light cannot escape Her.

She *is* light,
holder of all things,

deliverer of energy so pure
it heals all
Hands
Souls
Bodies

She is
Raw,
a truly magnificent creation,
her body bursting,
with divine wisdom,
her divinity unbound by the clothes She wears.

She is
All things
Complex
full of dualities and paradoxes
Intelligent
Seductive
Supple and firm
Fierce
Intimidating
And
Gentle

A Great Force
Kind
Love personified

I met a womxn once
who was all things Holy,
capable of holding
the entire world in Her tender hands:
Divina
Guererra

Strong
like the smell of burning sage and copal
Powerful
Cleansing
Unforgettable

She
was God.

So I wonder

why She continues to be

the last to see

all that She is.

_____

Josie Valadez Fraire is a 22 year old Xicana/Indígena womxn, born in Boulder, Colorado and raised in Zacatecas, México/Boulder. She recently graduated from the University of Colorado Boulder with two Bachelor's Degrees in Psychology and Ethnic Studies with a Certificate in Women and Gender Studies. She is an activist, writer/researcher, educator, and community worker that is passionate about serving marginalized communities, particularly working with youth and womxn in the Black, Brown, and/or Indigenous community. Josie works to create decolonial, culturally-affirming, and liberating educational spaces for youth in Denver and beyond.

Love Is My Revolution by Hannabah Blue

Sometimes the travesties in the world form clouds over my head,
plunging me into darkness.
The injustices crowd me in,
overwhelm me and back me into a corner,
shove me back into the closet,
and conceal me in light colored skin.
I have been told:
if you are not angry,
you are not paying attention.
But the more attention that I pay,
the more I have to learn,
the more I need to give,
the more I am called to do,
the harder I must fight,
and the angrier I become.
But so much anger can consume you,
pushing you to the point where it seems like there is never enough.
I put my hands out to separate those clouds,
tear them apart,
and yet the light behind
shines too brightly that it blinds me.
I start to feel that what I am doing is not enough:
never enough to stop the injustices that happen to us;
never enough to keep our children safe;
never enough to right the wrongs of the world;
never enough.
So what is my part?
And what can I do that is enough?
Because never enough becomes: I am never going to make a difference;

becomes: how am I ever going to do this?
becomes: this is hopeless;
becomes: I am not even going to try.

With the weight of trying to change the world on my shoulders,
I lean forward,
sweating and breathing hard.
The muscles in my arms fill with the blood
that pulsates through my veins from the pounding in my chest.
And I realize:
what is change in the world,
without love in my heart?
I cannot fix everything outside of my body.
But when my heart murmurs as an infant born premature,
when my recessive genes carry dormant lupus disease,
and while I wage warfare against the demons of depression in my head,
I win battles everyday
and love is my revolution.

I want a baby.
Every time I see a kid,
my uterus cries,
my ancestors screaming through me to do better by their children,
keeping our people alive,
not just surviving,
but thriving.
And I know that babies are not conceived from just love or want.
But if they were,
this world would be a better place.
So before I can make the outside a better space for them,

let me start right here.
Love is my revolution.

So when you are thinking of all the people you want to help out there,
do not forget about the one right here.
Circle your life with love and health.
Let that be your revolution.
We can build fortresses in our homes, bedrooms, or in our own skin.
Our families, lovers, and children can know the love that we did not,
filling a cup that has run dry,
and been emptied for so long
so that we can swim together in healing waters for the rest of our lives.
Each act, each word can add a single but solid drop.

And my love, we can stop the cycles of abuse with a kiss.
We can heal the wounds of historical trauma while making love.
We can reoccupy our bodies,
reclaim them from those who have ravished Native women.
We can fight wars against genocide from our bedside.
We can drop bombs of butterflies in our stomachs.
We can stage demonstrations on cool Sunday mornings,
between coffee and brunch,
me reading my books and you watching cartoons.
Revolutions can be gentle, calm, comforting.
Your touch can undo the decades of self-doubt and guilt.
We will hold hands,
instead of holding arms.
And as we braid our fingers,
we can unravel the shame from our souls for being gay.
Colonization becomes coloring books.

Homophobia becomes a safe home.
And racism becomes reading bedtime stories,
loving our children unconditionally
and not alienating them for who they love,
for love is the answer.
And that we have it
should be celebrated
just as much as this touch.
Our battle cries will be words spoken in giggling whispers,
sweet nothings that echo deep in the chambers of our hearts
to the beating rhythms.
When I stare into your eyes and time stops,
I can go back to before wars were waged on our love.
This is my revolution
with forehead kisses strapped to my hips
and carrying long embraces as my weapons.
I march into the future,
not to forget the past,
but to build from it and set the stage for our children,
and their children,
and their children.
So they do not have to endure these battles.
And love can be their landscape
instead of their revolution.

I Don't Want to be Sick Anymore by Hannabah Blue

I don't want to be sick anymore.
You tell me my wide smile is a disorder,
my deep laughs are a sickness,
and the connection with my Dad is not real.
And I know that when I am up,
I am up.
And when I am down,
I am down.
But it is the ups that keep me from being down.
And if you took away these ebbs and flows,
I would be a flat line.

But I don't want to be sick anymore.
I do not want to be a slave to these pills,
a puppet on anti-psychotic strings:
one to smile,
one to cry,
one to sleep,
and one to numb the pain of their tight grips on my wrists,
cutting off the blood flow and turning my hands blue.

I am Blue.
But I cried the day I found out that meant sad.
I am Blue but I did not know it until you told me.
I am Blue.
But when I show the colors of my rainbow,
you try to strip me back to just one hue.
I am Blue.
But I don't want to be sick anymore

Can we think of a world
where my veins are aquamarine,

like the water of life,
where the lumps in my throat are turquoise stones
protecting the breaths I exhale
inhale
my tears are drops of cyan and I am sighing?

I am Blue.
But that is only because the lenses that you have
cannot see the complexity of the colors in my soul.
Instead of 3D glasses,
you have a tint that flattens.
And you only see my fire as a weak blue flame.

But my warmth glows and grows crimson.
So I am Red.
The shine on my cheeks are rosy as I smile.
I am Red.
And my hair shows streaks of auburn in the sun.
I am Red.
The freckles marooned on my skin,
each a reminder of my blessings from the Creator.

I am Red and I am Blue.
But I will not let you tell me that I am sick anymore.

Back to Black and White by Hannabah Blue

What is black and white and red all over?
No it is not a newspaper
and no it is not a zebra that has been sunburnt.

It is a re-colonized,
re-integrated,
re-assimilated,
re-discriminated
Native American.
Native and American
but not Native to America:
the land of the free
or the land of the
break down those who welcomed you;
land of the
build upon the backs of those enslaved;
land of the
only let those with material wealth rise;
land of the
black and white.

I feel like I am being colonized all over again,
like it is black and white,
as half Native and half white,
as half Native and half American.
My clan Tla'as'chi'i is Red Bottom,
the Red palm,
the red identity of this Dine' woman
in my left side where my heart resides
my left side,
where my free, art, song, poem, dance, music, feeling, love,
love, love;

in contrast to my America,
my white,
is my right
where my brain, control, thoughts, logic, judgment, actions,
error, error, error.

But no,
both sides make up me.
Red blood runs in my veins throughout my body.
When I eat the food of Mother Earth,
it nourishes me from my head to my arms, to my legs, to my feet.
Native American:
black and white
but Red all over,
colorful, fluid, dynamic, a canvas of life.
Various aspects sprinkled upon this spirit of mine,
created and gifted to me by the Great Spirit.
I am animal, human, woman, biracial, Native, Dine', and gay.

You see as if the rainbow of my identity
stands in contrast to the black and white of your world,
in contrast to the white pews of church,
in contrast to the black gown of the priest,
tainting, dirtying, corrupting, damning
"kill the Indian but save the man."
Back to black and white.

What about the middle,
the inbetween,
the grey space?
What about the Red?
I have been de-colorized and re-colonized,
the black fingers of the devil that you say I have been touched by.

You say
I am gay because I am not a Christian
and I am not a Christian because I am gay.
You say
I am not a Christian because I believe in hozho
and I believe in hozho because I am not a Christian.
You say
I am gay because I am Navajo
and I am Navajo because I am gay.
Back to black and white.

But Mother Earth teaches us
tolerance, acceptance, equality, balance, hozho
and white,
the absence of all colors,
and black,
the presence of all.
We are one and the same.
We are black and white and Red all over.

I am more than my sexuality.
The rainbow of my identity speaks to the complexity of my
life.
Yes, I am gay.
But I am also a poet, a writer, a teacher, a trainer, an educator,
a singer, a caretaker, a good samaritan, a donor, a volunteer, a
patient, a client, a liver, a dyer, a lover, a hater, a beauty, a
beast, a sister, a niece, an aunt, a girlfriend, a granddaughter,
and a daughter,
your daughter.
I am still your daughter.
But you are stuck in the black and white.

For two years,
you have been stuck in the black and white,

not being able to see past it.
I feel like I am being colonized all over again:
Back to black and white.

I am still your daughter
and I listen to your favorite songs.
I talk to you,
laugh with you,
cry with you,
as if we are living lives entwined but in different dimensions
moving along in the same spaces,
yet worlds apart,
analog in a digital space
or digital in an analog space.
Back to black and white

You will not hear me,
so I put these words as prayers to reach you
through the Great Spirit, the Creator, our God.
I pray just the same as you do.
We are one and the same:
Black and White and Red all over.

Hannabah Blue is Diné (Navajo), originally from Kirtland, New Mexico. Ms. Blue has a breadth of experience working in public health, particularly addressing health disparities affecting Native and LGBTQ+ communities. Currently, as a Consultant with John Snow, Inc., she provides technical assistance nationwide on various public health projects. Previously, she has supported organizations regionally and nationally in improving tribal health as the Public Health Services Project Manager at the American Indian Public Health Resource Center and as a capacity building assistance specialist at the National Native American AIDS Prevention Center.

Ms. Blue has an undergraduate degree in broadcast journalism and in gender and sexuality studies from New York University and a Maternal and Child Health Epidemiology Graduate Certificate focusing on Native women through the University of Arizona. She earned a Master of Science degree from the Harvard School of Public Health, with concentrations in women, gender, and maternal and child health.

I Am Native American by Tywania Holly

I am Native American
and I come from a large community
full of brothers and sisters.
I look in the mirror
and see a warrior
ready to fight for what is right.
I belong to the red and white mesas
that surround me in my sleep.
I dream of the past,
as my ancestors suffered
through misery and pain
caused by the new-comers
who we knew little about.
I hear my ancestors' cries
of sorrow
from the wounds they inflicted,
coloring their brown skin
red.
They showed us
how little they cared.

I know this by the many stories
that have been passed down
from generation to generation
in shi hoogan
by my chee.
I was even told of the large land
that we once had
way before it was taken
by the Naakáí and Bilagáanas.
Before,
our land spread across the four corners

Ha'a'aah
Shádi'ááh
E'e'aah
Náhookos
The sacred ruins can prove my point.

While the heat tans my brown skin,
I begin to blend into the red mesas.
As I stand at the cliff
with the cool breeze pulling my hair back,
it reminds me of how the eagles flew
across Shizhé'é's light blue skin
as he looks down upon Shimá,
who holds me in her arms
never letting go.
I might fly away.

Soon,
I will become a real warrior,
the next one in my family
with turquoise wrapped around my neck and wrists,
my hair tied up into a Tsiiyeel,
my eyes looking up at the dark skies
that are brightened by the several suns
and a full moon,
while the coyotes howl in the distance.

I am the beating drum
that blends with the pounding feet
that hit the burning soft light brown ground
as singing voices echo throughout the bare land.
All known people surround all kinds of dancers
who praise the lord
in their beautiful swaying moves.
That shows the image of a new generation afoot,

a new time,
a brand new start.

I will always remember the light touch of juice
that slowly drips down the dark meat
from the first bite.
I can still smell mutton expand across my homeland.
The sounds of laughter echo through my ears
of my family,
grandmas,
grandpa,
uncles,
aunts,
and so on.
As they laugh,
I can also hear the sounds of the fire
crackling underneath the handmade rock stove
that sits outside under a nearby tree.
This is where the butchering began.
It has always been in our small village of the Hollys.

I belong to my nation,
fore I am a Dine
and a strong warrior.
I grasp my language in my hands,
never letting go.
If I do,
I will lose everything that I am.
Even if I am hundreds of miles away from home,
I will always remember who I am.
I belong to the Water Edge clan
and the Coyote clan.
This is who I am
and this is who I will always be.
No one can take me away from what I am.

No matter what happens,
I will always remember
that I am a Native American,
a Navajo!
Ah éhee'!

Ty Holly (15th old Navajo): I'm a 15 year old student who loves to write poetry about racism, my culture, and my own life. Although I live in Denver, I grew up in Farmington, New Mexico, surrounded by the Four Sacred Mountains. I may seem like someone who does not have anything to say, but I have more to say than you think. Just listen to my poems and you will see the real me.

Walking by Jozer

I got that special type of walk,
the type of walk
your daddy used
when he first talked to your mama
type of walk.
Yeah,
I got that special type of lean,
so smooth,
you'd think I'm cruising a low-rider
on Cinco de Mayo.
See,
I've been working on my walk for a while now,
ever since I was a little chavalito.
I can recall my father
walking me through the process
at an early age.
He would say,
"Walking
is one of the simplest ways
you could show someone your freedom.
See,
the first step to being enslaved
is to actually get caught!
Why do you think Martin Luther King Jr
and Cesar Chavez
spent all that time marching!?
You have to stay on your toes,
mijo.
This system has interesting ways
of turning a man into a slave."
If you asked my father for a ride,
he would tell you to walk.

After crossing the desert for a better life,
he sees my walk to any Open Mic
as an easy stroll through the park.
Walking in my father's footsteps
has taught me
that if you love something,
you will do anything you can to get to it.
Your feet will get you there
if you allow them to.
My father walks
with the determination of an immigrant,
like his children will starve
if he doesn't walk fast enough,
like there are immigration agents
chasing after him.
He is America's worst nightmare,
a bad dude in a foreign country.
I always wanted to walk just like him.
But I always seem to take the wrong steps,
walking in and out of jail,
pacing in my cell
like a caged ocelot.
These must have been the ways
you get enslaved
my father talked about.
It all started in the seventh grade
when doctors explained to my parents
why I walked with a slight limp.
My right leg was shorter than the left,
forcing me to apply most of my body weight
on the right side.
I developed a walk
that would quickly label me a thug.
I guess the inequalities I was exposed to
finally drenched through my clothes

and into my bones.
So now,
I walk
like I got a wounded knee,
like the structure
holds me down by my back pockets.
Saggy jeans are one of the side effects
left over from my oppression.
When you walk with this much weight
at an early age,
your steps
begin to sound like ticking bombs,
with the type of walk
that'd make someone
move out the way,
the type of walk
that'd make a cop want to follow you.
In 2012,
Treyvon Martin was murdered
for having the same walk as me.
Treyvon was only 17.
They asked me why I cried
because he walked just like me,
because he was just like me!
He was still perfecting his own walk,
still getting use to the feeling
of walking in a black man's shoes.
This is the reason
why boys like us
never achieved social mobility.
How can we climbed the ladders of class
if we can't even walk through our neighborhoods
without feeling like someone is chasing after us.
But I'll risk it all
to show my son

and the rest of the chavalitos in the world
that we can walk to a better future
instead of having to walk away from everything,
that if we all walk at the same time,
the weight of our steps
would force the world to flip its rotation.
So,
stand up
and walk with me.
We have the world at our feet.
I think it's time
that we exercise our freedom.

43 by Jozer

Have you seen this picture?
Have you seen this picture?
"In this picture,
Jose was only seven,
the same age as his son.
At this age,
he was loud,
could sing any tune on the radio,
and as you can see,
he refused to wear clothes.
I love this picture.
He is so innocent and full of LIFE,
so comfortable in his own skin."
My mother speaks the most beautiful words.
She loves to read through the memoirs
she has captured in our family photo albums.
Each image and elaborate story she would share with my son.
When she is not reminiscing,
she loves to watch the news: "Primer Impacto!"
She says those news anchors are just a bunch of chismosos
like the women in Juarez.
I smile
but you cannot hold a smile for long
when you watch the news in Spanish.
It is all blood and civil war,
neocolonialism
and drug trafficking.
On this day,
they are filming live from Iguala Guerrero, Mexico:
a city known best for its beautiful flags and missing children,
all 43 of them.
It has been one year since the mysterious disappearance of

(interrupted)
News correction:
It has been one year since the kidnapping and murder of
43 students from Ayotzinapa,
stolen by Mexican police and burned by a dump.
This is what happens when Brown children get too loud in public places.
We turn them into crime scenes,
burn news segments into ashes,
and reduce them to their baby pictures.
"On today's episode,
we will be speaking live with two mothers of the disappeared."
Both women are tired and soft-spoken.
So used to their words going unheard,
they never imagined they would reach stardom
pleading for the lives of their vanished sons.
"Ha pasado un ano."
It has been one year since our sons were taken.
Our hands have grown weary from praying the Rosary,
our fingers still paper cut
bleeding from holding on too tight to their last photos.
We are shaking
not from fear
but from rage.
We want them back alive
because that's the way they took them.
We are starving for answers,
so will you please help us?
"Ha visto al muchacho en esta foto?
Ha visto al muchacho en esta foto?
Have you seen my son?
Here is his picture."
And no one ever will.
As I watch the news,
I cannot help but notice the similarities

between these women and my mother.
They all know the meaning of sacrifice so well.
So I ask a question,
no trigger warning,
I just shoot!
"Mama,
which picture would you choose if that was me?"
She does not answer.
The wells underneath her eyes give me the only answer I need.
No mother should ever be burdened with choosing the last picture
the world will remember their child by.
To this day,
those women still believe those boys are alive,
walking down the streets of Mexico,
wailing the names of their stolen sons.
They are modern day Lloronas,
holding headshots full of headshots.
There is blood on the president's hands.
Here I stand telling the story like it is foreign,
like our news is not flooded
with shots of Brown and Black boys being shot.
So let me ask you a question,
have you seen these pictures?
Have you seen these pictures?
If you have not,
all you have to do is open your eyes.

You Are Not the Father by Jozer

The results are in
in the case of America Christopher Columbus:
You are not the father!
I am writing this poem on Columbus Day,
picking at scabs from old wounds
that have yet to heal,
reading old history textbooks for inspiration.
If there is anything more painful
than an old white guy telling your story,
it is when it is wrongfully told.
I still remember the first time I learned his name.
My teacher's words sounded more like a rifle,
"Christopher Columbus discovered America."
In that moment,
I felt the Thunder Beings crack the sky.
I was in first grade
and even then,
I understood that something was missing.
So,
I raised my hand
and somehow it felt like an Indian revolt,
like I was shooting wooden arrows into the mouth of a steel
canon.
"What about the Indians?
How can you discover someone
when Mother Earth already spoke their name into existence?"
Mr. Washington's eyes turned into smallpox blankets
ready to exterminate any question that I had.
Well,
the Indians were just a bunch of heathens,
undressed and uncivilized.
Suddenly,

our classroom turned into the Battle at the Little Bighorn.
The ancestors said,
"Today is a good day to die."
I will be damned
if I let these fools lie.
But I was 7 years old,
excluded from Thanksgiving dinner,
scoldings I received felt like a massacre at Sand Creek,
like braids being cut off at boarding school.
They say the only good Indian is a dead Indian.
So they cut off our hands
if we did not bring enough gold.
"If you really wish to exterminate the savages
you must start with their children
because nits make lice
and lice are bloodthirsty."
But here is the irony:
when Columbus first encountered the Tainos,
he gave us the name Indios,
meaning in God,
for God's children.
Someone please explain to me
why we worship a man
who killed angels.
I guess he read the Bible
the same way he read map coordinates,
with his eyes closed.
Yet today,
we still celebrate the world's biggest mistake.
The truth is
Columbus never even stepped foot on what we call America.
His bloody spirit still lives on:
in the hungry trigger fingers of police officers
killing Indians at a higher rate
than any other racial group in America;

through oil pipelines
that stretch themselves to our reservations,
polluting our water supply.
America,
is there not enough blood underneath your fingernails already?
You have tried so hard
to bury us underground.
But you forgot
that we were seeds.
Our red tree will still blossom.
You will never cut us down.

Jozer is a professional Poet, Actor, and Hip-Hop artist based in Denver, CO. His work tackles tough political issues such as immigration discrimination, racial inequalities, and police brutality. His work has landed him features on HBO, PBS, Button Poetry, TED Talks, and has been reviewed by the L.A Times and American Theatre Magazine. He also placed 3rd in the Individual World Poetry Slam in 2013, and has placed in the top 15 last two years. When he is not performing, he educates and inspires youth teaching poetry and teatro courses to students of all ages. If you are interested in working or contacting Jozer, you can email jozerg7@gmail.com for further information.

Just Get Over It by Nizhonii Mitchell

"Just get over it.
That is how life is.
Life is a challenge."
Just get over it?
You do not know the struggles I have went through.
"Why do Native Americans wear silly costume?"
"All you Indians get into college for free,
that's not fair."
"Can you make it rain by dancing?"
What do these statements mean?
Silly costumes,
getting into college for free?
My regalia is not a Halloween costume.
Even on Instagram they post,
"White girls rock headdresses."
These women do not know what a headdress means,
as they walk around my school calling themselves savages.
Stereotypes can influence one's identity.
Stereotypes have changed me:
not speaking up in class,
even if I hear the wrong
or missing information in a history book.
History,
what is history to other people's eyes
when they make the wasichu man look like a hero?
So I just can't get over it and move on.
This is my culture.
Each stitch,
each design,
each jingle on my dress
is Nizhonii,
beauty.

When I dance,
I am dancing for my ancestors,
my ancestors who fought for my tribe
and for me to be
where I am today.

Nizhonii Mitchell: 2016-17 Denver Indian Center Princess

A Friend by reMARKable

James is a friend
without fatherly guidance
and most importantly,
love.
He isn't the first
wishing to diminish from earth
so he can be soaring above.
I swear he's not okay.
See,
I've been to his house,
single mother,
empty fridge,
not even cheese for the mouse.
Then I asked where his dad was.
He said either doing drugs,
selling them,
or growing old and weak in a cell.
Mark,
I want to see him
but if so,
I know my mother would catch a beating from hell.
I'm in need of some help
'cause to another friend like you
this stuff isn't easy to tell.
See,
James is a friend
with no one to look up to
except for life
'cause it just knocked him on the pavement again.
He tries to get up
but depression is constantly weighing on him,
along with the fact that his dad

is going to visit soon,
coming straight out the pen.
It's been one long year
so mixed emotions arise inside him,
like an early morning sun
just above the horizon,
like "he's the best.
Actually,
no my dad sucks.
I mean,
Mark,
the last time I saw him
he left my house in handcuffs.
Sure,
he went to jail
but I'm talking about my family
'cause he left us
with the memories of broken promises
that bonded like a chain
and left our wrists shackled up.
And the only key to release for us
is forgiveness,
easier said than done.
Yeah,
James is a friend,
moments away from swinging fists full of hatred at his father
'cause he chose to neglect his son.
There he is,
"that man,"
walking out of the penitentiary;
yeah,
"that man,"
who when I was in elementary,
disregarded each one of my needs so blatantly;
of course,

"that man,"
who actually looks the same as me.
It's not in the sense of resemblance
but in the sense that our eyes reflect the early loss of our
innocence.
That's when the tears flow
and kill the fiery rage
that evokes my desire for vengeance.
Fists of hatred
quickly turn to open hands of love.
Then there's an instant connection,
as two broken hearts become one,
and this was all accomplished with one hug.
Now,
James sees his father not as enemy
because he has now been awakened to the fact
that forgiveness is not for his dad
but something he really needs.
All this time,
he has been asleep.
James now knows
that if you want to continue on being hurt,
the price you pay is your inner peace.

Hands Up by reMARKable

Do I have a place in this world?
Or am I just a waste of oxygen?
Because I feel like their main intention
is just trying to lock me in a box and then
do the same to the rest of my people.
These preconceived beliefs of me always infest my cerebral,
step on my neck 'til it's feeble,
then lock my hands up.
You blasted on my bro
even with his hands up.
You put us in handcuffs
and blast us with damn guns.
I can only imagine the stories
that I'll be telling my grandsons
like,
"License and registration
with no sudden movements
when you're reaching to grab 'em!"
But I need to thank God for blessing me
with this pen and paper
that is with me when I'm spitting out my stress,
the same paper that will make sure your excessive aggression
and power tripping
is addressed.
When all the thoughts in my mind are regathered,
these words are like a knife or dagger,
sharp enough to penetrate the very stitchin' on your vest.
Know that we're demanding respect
now.
This isn't a request.
Because so many have died
for just a bit of respect.

reMARKable or Mark Gutierrez (Denver Hip Hop Artist & Poet) is a recent graduate of La Academia and first year student at Metropolitan State University at Denver. He picked up rapping at the age of 12. From then on, Mark has practiced and developed his craft until he was comfortable enough to share his material. His main purpose is to express and be original, all without sacrificing the complexity of his rhyme scheme. Give his rhymes one listen and it'll be clear that this kid has reMARKable flows.

back to the beginning by Tanaya Winder

sometimes i wish we could start back
at the beginning. turn our existence into a videotape
call it *Life*. then push *Life* into a VCR.
press PLAY then PAUSE and get the chance to
REWIND with our image still on screen
watching everything that ever meant anything reverse
with the push of a finger.

if we could press REWIND
the wrinkles on these God given shells would smooth
into soft unscathed skin. we'd awaken from tombs,
arise from the earth like trees living to become seeds,
and i guess that means as babies we'd go back into our
mother's wombs.

if we could press REWIND
mothers or fathers who abandoned
their daughters or sons wouldn't walk away but return,
run backwards turning towards their children.
then they'd never have to look into eyes
that ever saw them as unworthy of keeping.
history wouldn't repeat, but instead fold into itself
like disease-ridden blankets rolling themselves back up
like yo-yos returning to the hands that made those hateful
gestures
in the first place. battles wouldn't end
in bloodshed, but instead a ride off into a sun rising
with warriors always returning from war
or boarding schools with their hair flowing behind them in
lengths of rivers.

REWINDing, would mean

Cafe Cultura

handing in our diplomas & going back to school
to unlearn all the lessons ever taught to us. we'd start
books at their ending, unstring sentences into letters until
all we were left with was sound waiting
to come out of our mouths. like my friend Angel,
his would open to fountain gallons of vodka
from liver, his throat would spill it back into bottle
after bottle after bottle after bottle
that he'd set back onto the shelves of a liquor store
he'd walk out of in a line so straight it'd lead him
to the day Angel's father cut off his wings when he left him,
fatherless, falling asleep on a bench.

REWINDing,
he'd unfreeze to death as warmth re-entered
his body convulsing not in dry heaving but reheating
detoxing into calm as snowflakes would slowly rise back up to
the sky.
the kind of miracle time travel – imagine,
needles sucking poisonous drugs from addicted veins, pills
un-dissolving into wholeness being pushed back into containers
fitting just right. everything would be all right.
especially for our youth who contemplated taking their own
lives
or committed suicide would feel blood flow back into open
cuts,
their veins pulsing with life that knows it's worth saving
so much that determined hands repeatedly pull away razors
from wrists until every scar slowly disappeared leaving behind
no trace,
not even the memory. and every fist that hit someone in rage
or abuse
would loosen into outstretched arms to call you home
instead of the bullet shaped holes being shot into bodies

making their way back into the guns or mouths
that shot them in the first place.

if we could REWIND
maybe i could remember
if i ever said anything to hurt Angel.

if we could REWIND,
my Angel would be able to fly
backwards, defy gravity, lift himself up and
life would be breathed back into him
as he unwrapped the rope from his neck
to inhale sweet and ever expanding air into his chest.

if we could REWIND
i could tell Angel, over & over *i loved you*
and it would always always start with –
you, alive & well and not me.
i'd give up every poem i have ever spoken,
have my mouth call back each and every one of them
from your ears back into my pen
's failed attempts at putting back together
all the splintered pieces of our
hearts our hearts our hearts
our hearts staring at a blank page,
wishing we could

begin again.

Sonnet MCLXXXI by Tanaya Winder
for the murdered & missing Indigenous women on Turtle Island

Not when or where but how, did we lose you,
in between Last Seen _____ the words become elegy
echoing sidewalks and streets. Hand out your picture to
strangers. Post it on Post Office bulletin boards: Missing
as if it were destination, a place one goes
to disappear in invisible cities. Except there's no hero like
in the movies. No ads, mainstream coverage, or TV shows
to show our story. Are we invisible if no one knows, why?
When 1,181 women were taken, did eyes cease to have vision
or pay attention to a body being swallowed up?
Those left behind who remember you continue on a mission,
an endless search of the cities in which we loved
(and love) you. We will never forget. We demand for you
action, words, even a poem that ends: your lives matter, too.

ten little indians by Tanaya Winder
> *one in three Native American or Alaska Native women will be raped at some point in their lives*

sometimes the story is told differently: *one little, two little, three little indians*
or not told at all. most know one story about indian boys torn
between reservation and cities. tradition:
bear   root   sage   drumbeats
history and what's left?
bear turned to beer

dances to drunken driving, the stereotypical drunken indian
and maybe we're all gambling our lives away *four little,*
five little, six little indians and it's not just the boys,
but our princesses too. per capita
has made some greedy. for, blood
quantum has turned us needy,
craving to make ourselves whole.

babies born into broken wombs, in a community
where ten little indian boys should learn
how to be men. instead, we ask:
do they remember?   how
to touch a woman

with respect. the old dances taught us,
    she   chooses   you *seven little, eight little, nine little indians,*
ten little indian boys   sit on the bus listening –
their older cousins joke and tease, "see…
that girl in baggy sweats about to get on?
she had a train pulled on her this weekend."

they laugh, the little indian boys do, not knowing someday
not too long from now men will gather around a fire

singing forty-nine songs about

love. maybe their fathers' never taught them
how to touch her, that loving her didn't mean taking her
blacked out where she wakes up not remembering, not
remembering:

> *ten little, nine little, eight little indians,*
> *seven little, six little, five little indians,*
> *four little, three little, two little indians.*
> *one little indian boy.*

Tanaya Winder is a writer, educator, motivational speaker, and performance poet from the Southern Ute, Duckwater Shoshone, and Pyramid Lake Paiute Nations. She grew up on the Southern Ute Indian reservation and attended college at Stanford University where she earned a BA in English and the University of New Mexico where she received an MFA in creative writing. Since then she has co-founded As/Us: A Space for Women of the World and founded Dream Warriors, an Indigenous artist management company. She guest lectures, teaches creative writing workshops, and speaks at high schools, universities, and communities internationally. Tanaya writes and teaches about different expressions of love (self-love, intimate love, social love, community love, and universal love); she is an advocate of heartwork and believes everyone has a gift they've been placed on this earth to share.

Water Is Life by Lucille Left Hand Bull

Water is sacred.
It is the bringer of life.
Oil is death.
Mother earth is being bled,
stripped of her sacred medicine.
With each oil spill,
she gets more sick.
Rivers turn black with oil,
polluting our water,
contaminating our soil.
By digging so deep,
we are killing our mother earth,
slowly poisoning her veins
in a slow brutal death.
But we only hurt ourselves.
How are we going to survive without water?

I stand up
and fight to protect my future.
I say no to the Dakota Access Pipeline.
I stand with Standing Rock.
Being a kid,
I am learning that I have to stand up
to protect my rights as a human.
I have the right
to not have oil
be spilled into the rivers
or on the land.
I want to survive,
to keeping having life.

We,

Native youth,
bring great medicine to the people.
Our words hold strong prayers
to stop the pipeline.
We have the power to change this world,
by not using oil
or other fossil fuels.
We can use solar energy.
We can heal mother earth
and protect our water
out of love.

Listen to my voice.
Stop doing this to our water.
Please stop letting this happen.
Stand with us
and our relatives
in Sacred Stone Camp,
Oceti Sakowin,
Red Warrior Camp,
and All Nations Camp.
Native warriors unite.

Lucille "Lucy" Left Hand Bull is a youth that resides in Denver, Colorado by way of South Dakota and New Mexico. She is a 9 years old Indigenous poet and activist. She is Rosebud Sioux (Sicangu Oyate Lakota) and Xicana (Mexica). She found her voice with poetry, which helped her overcoming many obstacles like bullying. She enjoys performing hand drum songs and loves the color purple.

What Is Beautiful? by Alejandro Jimenez

A few months ago, I bought a shirt
from a cashier that was wearing enough makeup
to bury her ancestors' brown skin
for the next 500 years.

She hid her smile behind western ideals of beauty.
She looked at me through fake eyes.
Her heart
felt like
US treaties with Native Americans,
Broken.

I offered to help gather the pieces
and shape them into turquoise necklace
to place around her mother's desert walk
to get to this country,
but she refused.

The next day,
I learned that a woman
gave English names to all of her four little girls.
She figures this way,
they will face less discrimination
if they didn't have a name that sounded like mine.

"The darkness of their skin," she says
"will be an asset to their future employers."

She speaks to them in her broken English
because she wants them to forget the past.

I know a kid,

that is haunted by the words he used to curse
his mother for not being white,
and for not having him born in this country.
See, he was undocumented AND afraid.
So when the policeman asked to see his ID,
he just pointed at the sun and ran.

He figured he could catch one of those rays
and slide down to his little Mexican town,
into a Mexican springtime
when he would run up and down paved streets
catching butterflies for his blind great grandmother.
Then would explain to her
about how they were first an egg
then a caterpillar,
a chrysalis that sprouted symmetrical wings
and how if you were careful enough,
you could use the powder on their wings to paint your face.

She would smile real big,
say
mijo,
paint my face the color of yesterday,
and take me back to the time
to the time of the revolution,
And
mijo,
Did you know that I sung for the governor, the president, and Pancho
Villa's calvary?

She would smile real big,
and rock back-and-forth in her chair
and she would smile
and she would rock back-and-forth
and she would break into tears,

simultaneously breaking into her favorite song:

Si Adelita quisiera ser mi novia,
si Adelita fuera mi mujer,
la pasearía por cielo y por mar
por cielo y por mar en un buque de guerra
y por tierra en un tren militar.

1993—
is the time he wants to go back to
Instead,
he is caught between the sun and the policeman chasing him
Now,
now he has met America
and he is not sure if he believes all the things they told him about her.
For example: everybody is treated equal in America,
you can be yourself there in America.

You see now,
now he has met a cashier,
and a mother,
that treat their own skin as if it was a sickness.

He has seen his family eagerly going to church,
hoping to find something that makes them believe in themselves.
But he figures that
Jesus!
He only walked on water.

We built cities on lakes,
like Tenochtitlan,

carved beauty out of mountain tops like Machu Picchu,

dug our hands under them,
held them to the sky
and told their *God*:
This is what heaven looks like!

We are not ruins discovered by archeologists.
We are temples.
Our most precious artifacts nestled inside of our chests.

But I rarely expose them because we have been told
that they may not be enough for you.

So, we insist in using language and makeup
to cover them up
and we forget to remember,
that you,
like my grandmother's smile,

You my friends,
are very beautiful!

When I Think About My Grandma by Alejandro Jimenez

When I think about my grandmother,
I remember needle and thread
flower patterns on pillows
scarred fingers
patient eyes
careful weaving hands.

When I think about my grandmother,
I remember the container full of clothes
she would balance on her head,
down the steep hill of the canyon to the river.

Carrying a small bag of soap,
I would struggle to keep up.

Downstream, people did not hear the roaring river.
They listened to my grandmother's rhythmic movements
of washing clothes against the rocks.
Amazed, I watched and listened.

On her 64th birthday,
we sat under the lemon tree in her backyard.
It was a sunny Mexican Sunday in June.
It felt like a day on the beach.
That tree, I can remember
when I used to hold a stick
with my arm and almost touch its top.

We sat,
music playing.

Cafe Cultura

My grandmother requests La Misma Gran Senora by Jenni Rivera,
a song about a woman telling her lover that she will still be great even if he left.
The owner of the sound system
hooks up a microphone
and we take turns singing songs.

My grandmother,
I can remember holding her hand
while navigating the busy streets of the big city 40 mins away.
I cannot help but think how her house does not have dirt floors anymore
like when she raised me in it.

I cannot help but think how tall the lemon tree is now.

My grandmother is complex.
I have learned more about being a man
by being attentive to her quiet nature
than I have from kissing
my uncles on their cheeks.

On this Sunday afternoon,
my grandmother sits next to her best friend,
who by default has become my auntie,
mi tia Ramona
They egg each other to drink more and to sing louder.
My grandmother sings El Columpio,
an older song usually accompanied by a saxophone, an accordion, and a 12 string Mexican guitar.
Her mouth embodies all those instruments plus more.
It talks about lovers pleading honesty for and from each other.

When she sings,

tears roll down her cheek.
We sing along.
Her voice breaks.
She looks at those present
and cries even harder.
Mi tia Ramona tells her to suck it up,
holds her beer up in the air and yells as loud as she can.

My grandmother laughs and keeps singing.

I cannot help but think what all she bore raising 9 children
in rural Mexico with a husband too macho to be loyal.

I wonder if she thinks of him when she is singing.

I am teary eyed now,
the river is zig zagging through my eyelashes,
not the canyon her and I used to walk down.

When the song ends,
we all clap.
We smile.
And we dance.
We dance under the lemon tree well past midnight,
until neighbors come joins us, citing our laughter as a reason
enough to crash the party
We dance until we are all tired of stomping on the ground
with our feet and beer has run out,
and people remember that tomorrow will be Monday.

That night, I hug my grandmother,
tell her I love her
she lets out a few tears,
just like when I call her from the US,
squeezes my hands

and tells me "gracias mijo".
I want to explain to her that I am the one that's thankful,
but I can't.
Choked up,
I sit under the lemon tree for a bit
and whisper the songs she sang.
I smile and cannot help but think
how my hands fit perfectly in hers
even now,
that I can touch the top of the lemon tree with a stick.

---

alejandro is spoken word poet, educator, avid distance runner and soccer fanatic from Colima, Mexico. Arriving in the United States as an undocumented immigrant, in 1995, and working as a farm worker for over 10 years in Oregon, he now resides in Denver, CO. Upon becoming the first member in his family to graduate from college he moved to the 'mile high city' to organize for immigrant rights. Now, he works with youth in Northside Denver. Alejandro understands the power of words and the liberation of speaking for oneself instead of being spoken for.

www.alejandropoetry.com

The Answer by Simako Marshall

"Hey Simako,
call the native gods."
"Simako,
do the rain dance."
"Do you get high with the Chief?"
"Where's the booze at Sim?
Are you drunk?"
Each day,
I went to school,
thinking the day was going to be cool,
until I ran into those fools.
For the 1st 2 years,
I tried to ignore them
because I thought the "jokes" would fade away.
I saw Elias get so angry,
I knew it was not okay.
They laughed at him because he was mad.
But some knew it was bad
seeing how their "jokes" hurt us.
I felt my Native pride fade away into the dust.
Some apologized
except one,
Paco the main one.
So fed up,
I was done.
His jokes were not cool,
not even fun.
He made me so angry,
I took it out at home.
He really damaged me in the dome.
Last year,
1st semester,

everything was the same,
nothing got better.
When we had a long term sub,
Paco decided to have some fun.
The sub laughed with him.
I wanted to run,
run so far
where I could disappear.
Thinking about if I should fight him.
No,
that isn't you Sim.
You are a lover,
not a fighter.
Do not add more fuel to the fire.
But aren't you tired?
You are getting so heated,
you are on fire.
Getting even is what you desire.
Going into the 2nd semester,
Paco was the same,
nothing got better.
Walking down the hall,
I was feeling proud and tall.
I saw him
and pinned him against the wall.
For too long,
I kept my anger in a ball.
It was time to unleash hell.
If I get in trouble,
oh well,
knowing he won't quit.
I am on a good path,
I need to stick with it.
Stay strong,
show him who is the better man.

You don't have to do it with your hands.
He has to know what he put me through,
beating him so bad was what I wanted to do.
I saw that he was finally scared
and told the assistant principal.
She pulled me out of class,
telling me the bad things Paco had done in the past.
He finally stopped at last.
We both lucked out
because the situation was going to get worse.
My anger was ready to burst.
It took me 4 years to find a way to make him stop.
I wasn't sure how I did it.
I am still lost.
The Threat of
Violence
Must
Have
Been
The
Answer.

It by Diego Florez

She saw life in the flower of her eye
She sees color in mine
Raging waves no love can deny
Shapes dance in place
Right before my eyes.
Watching true love really take place
Singing songs about her
Keep me together.
She holds me close on the far side of weather
Cold outside but we have warm love so good and so tender

I might be a bit crazy so it seems
I sew the seams of this reality
We start when you can see
All your soul can be.

Scratching the Surface by Diego Florez

So deep so deep
Bottomless
All the rocks have elevated
But still stay glued to the wall

So deep so deep
Oceans of perception
I feel at home in the retina
But know love carries light

So deep so deep
Intercept violet ray
Transformed into the words
We choose to say

So deep so deep
She was so deep
All I wanted to do was fall in

So deep so deep
She was a different scene
All she wanted was to be loved

So deep so deep

First, Second, Third, Fourth by Diego Florez

First the worst,
second the best,
third tells the truth,
and the fourth brings it round for the rest.

She could go tomorrow
To raise our children
We all wanna be parents
That will never end

Stayed sedated
You will get to where you are going
Everybody wants that feeling
Some people just can't get enough

Ain't got no water
we do have wine
If you got water you got wine
But ain't got water you ain't got wine

You lost the race
But you won the bet
Don't put all your eggs in one basket
Don't have a line so I'll sing it my best

Diego is an Observer, poet, artist, and musician from North Denver. He has been sharing his art as a career for about 3 years now. Cafe Cultura was one of the first open mics he ever went to. After seeing poets like Ara Cruz, Bobby Lefebre, and Innocencio Ox Mendoza, he was inspired to write his own poetry and do work in and for his community.

Blue Corn Woman by Eden Nicole

With cradle board on my back carrying this heavy load,
of being a woman on this red road,
the concrete shatters beneath my feet,
as I tread in truth I seek.

Pages of the past fluttering,
dripping memories that laid this foundation,
I am the harvester of life's creation.
I bring life in this sacredness.

Running across the sky,
my secrets ride on the back of the moon.
She,
bright and full,
is my emblem of happiness.

Roots of my soul reaching to the earth's core,
my blue corn woman was said to be at a time of war.
The good book claims my blood is that of false idols.
Truth is I come from the essence of the rain.
I return to this Eden as the drum beat balances my soul,
I bring the pain.

My voice pierces the sky with earth songs,
as I sand paint the colors of my heart on the back of butterfly
wings,
and thus she carries my dreams.

My shield of Turquoise greets the sun,
spirit guardian of three sacred boys.
Woman warrior am I,
with the revolution on the grinding stones,

taking back our mother,
and crashing the systematic thrones.

My spirituality rises in the east and whispers to the west,
as I scribe this story into my breast.
I inhale the elders in the north,
calling echoes,
my Indigenous bringing forth.
To the seeds we grant in the south,
emit the wisdom,
from my tongue,
teeth,
and mouth.

Forthcoming of my blue corn woman was said to be that at a time of war,
weaving the calendar,
blessing the ways in these final days,
500 years of prophecies reveal destiny's door.

In Lak Ech by Eden Nicole

I carry the sun for my sister,
as her pain becomes mine intuitively.
Different minds,
same eyes realize,
adhering souls with yucca fibers into the sky,
we scream this creed.

In Lak Ech…..you are the other me.

Cloning afflictions
and singing a symphony of pain
that turns into an epiphany of strength
makes us sisters,
a family we have chosen to be.

In Lak Ech….you are the other me.

Casting our prayers into the heavens
like thunder clashing to claim our divinity.
Offering our hearts layer by layer
like the water that cleanses sandstone,
creating the ability to plant positivity.

In Lak Ech….you are the other me.

Branching from the same seed,
cultivating life's fragility,
surpassing the struggle.
Healing by flower and song that is sweet poetry,
as we walk,
we walk in beauty.

In Lak Ech....you are the other me.

My Creator:
may the roots of my soul run deep into the sultry soil of this red earth,
embracing the horizon,
receiving the blessings of this feminine equality.
giving myself to you and my celestial beliefs.

Creator....In Lak Ech....you are the other me.

I Come From the Corn by Eden Nicole

I once used a term of endearment for my son:
"mijo,"
son,
child,
little one.
Then I was asked,
"So, you're MEXICAN now?!"

Oh, how my heart sank.
How could I be stereotyped,
when I conceived to break boundaries?
Of course,
I was Mexikah,
always was,
always will be.

But my soul's response was this:
Who are you to tell me what to be,
and I am not speaking hypothetically.
I come from the corn that was rooted into my DNA,
into your DNA that lyrically speaks through me universally.

I have been told,
you are never brown enough for the brown
and never red enough for the red.
You see,
I am neither here nor there,
neither brown nor red;
but created by both equally.

I have been Mexikah

since before the day my great grandfather rode horseback
alongside Pancho Villa.
I have been Mexikah
since before the conquest of new life drifted over seas,
with its effects rippling to multiple degrees.
I am the pyramids planted scientifically to exist amongst the
cosmos in harmony.

I am of generations of healers and weavers,
a woman of the San Filipe Pueblo, and Dine'.
I am the adobe that constructs the Pueblos and Hogans,
and the corn pollen offered at dawn.

I am my grandfather's finger prints left in the stars in the sky,
telling stories of how we came to be.
I am my grandmother's prayers,
my blood is that of migrant workers,
red earth carriers.
I am all that grows photosynthetically,
before being contaminated carcinogenically.
I am etchings of the 5th sun with its reasoning embedded into
my soul consciously.

I am a product of oppression,
chasing my histories denigrating paper trails.
I am a product of slaveries and massacres,
still my people rise to greet the sun.
I am a product of governmental prosecutions,
shedding my light on the lies.
I am a product of social movements and planetary revolutions,
therefore reconfirming my conclusions.

I am a woman of the San Felipe Pueblo,
a sacred woman,
a Dine' woman,

a strong woman,
a Mexikah woman,
an intellectual woman.
We call this a Chicana woman,
created by both brown and red equally.
I stand here a proud woman.

I come from the corn that was rooted into my DNA,
into your DNA that lyrically speaks through me universally.
So again I ask you,
who are to tell me what to be,
and I am not speaking hypothetically.

Born and raised in Denver, Eden merges her inspirations from her children with her Indigenous roots (Mexikah, Dine', and San Felipe Pueblo) to create spoken word. Through Groupo Tlaloc, Medicine Heart Dancers and Cafe Cultura, she is teaching her sons the traditions of their people; while also pursuing her Bachelor's degree in Environmental Sciences.

Imagine by Celeste Delgado

Imagine this:
a young girl is sitting in a classroom,
her shirt just a little big,
slides off her shoulder.
The teacher says,
"You need to change."
Girls cannot show their legs
or shoulders
because it is a distraction.
Yet no one teaches these boys
that just because a girl dressed a certain way
does not mean
you can get in their pants.

Imagine this:
a girl walks down the street
in some short shorts
and a tank top.
There are cars
full of men
that turn their heads
so they are no longer looking at the road.
People honk
and yell as they drive passed this young girl.
Little does she know,
she is not alone.
There has been a man
following her for the past 20 blocks.
As soon as she is out of the public's view,
he robs her of her innocence.
She runs home
with a sea in her eyes

and tells her parents.
Their only reaction is,
"You shouldn't dress like that then…"

Girls are used,
taught
that we cannot dress a certain way
because the boys,
the men
will do things to you
that you are not ready to do.
Somehow it is our fault
that these boys,
these men
cannot keep their pets locked away.

This is to the men who follow young girls
until they are alone.
This is to the men
who follow women to the restroom at the bar.
This is to anyone who does not take responsibility,
who think it is okay to blame a woman
for what you have done to her.
This is to the young boys:
do not make the same mistake
these foolish men have made.
We are women,
not something you can just take,
because it looks good.

―――――――――――

My name is Celeste. I am 15 years old and I attend DSST College View High School.

Removing the Chains by Ara Cruz

In my world,
hip hop and history meet
as we
greet the rising sun and honor our mother with a drum beat.
See,
I carry my ancestors flower and song
long after the struggle to keep these traditions strong.
So I write with red and black ink
about those who came before me.
Ask me about my purpose on this earth,
and I'll probably start out with a story:

On a 524 year old journey
to find my way back to the circle,
I stumble
through a concrete jungle
of insanity,
full of despair and void of humanity.
I have no voice,
no face,
no name.
Shackled and chained
from my feet to my mind,
looking for a way out
but running out of time -
and in time,
money and violence occupy my thoughts.
I try to get up,
find myself caught,
trapped in a web of illusions and lies,
wanting to break out
and remove the red, white, and blue blindfold from my eyes.

This mental cage.
This mental cage.
Just then,
my nose is touched lightly by the sweet smell of copal and sage.
A smoking mirror appears,
and through it,
I travel into the deepest chasms of my spirit.
Sounds of drumming pass through the now smoke and steam filled air,
as danzantes emerge in the distance
to disrupt my once fixed stare.
Songs of healing arrive on the winds from the 4 directions,
seeking to create a lasting connection.
between my heart and my mind,
my being and the earth,
the raped, violated, and battered mother of my birth.
It is here that my consciousness starts to awaken,
and with persistence,
I am able to shed, little by little,
the layers of my enslaved existence.
The chains of colonization are falling from my brain.
For the first time in my life,
I am able to start ridding myself of the blindness
that has caused me so much strife.
I begin to cry,
tears flowing down my scarred face,
as I try to resist being consumed in this rat race.
I begin to sing and pray,
to sing and pray.
I ask the creator for strength and guidance to act in a good way.
Because it's like they say:
"La cultura cura,
ancient medicine,

embrace your identity and let the healing begin."
begin...
begin...
I begin
to hear my ancient voice,
see my timeless face,
and remember my true name.
As I touch this Red Road,
it starts to rain:
purpose, understanding, dignity
to nourish the seed that is
me,
me,
a Xicano who doesn't need permission to be free.
'Cause you see,
I will no longer live on my knees.
With my ancestors at my side,
I will stand
to fight the war and domination-driven occupier of this land,
I,
an Indigenous man.

For You by Ara Cruz

I wrote this poem for you.
Escribí ese poema para ti.

Porque eres una mujer inteligente y fuerte
y ya se que no fue suerte conocerte.

And when we first met,
I got lost in your gorgeous dark eyes,
surprised
'cause it was like trying to grasp the vastness of the evening sky.

See,
your beauty
is beyond breathtaking
because
you give it back to me
por tus ojos poderosos,
hechos por obsidiano.
Con solo una mirada,
puedes curarme de cualquier daño.

In fact,
the darkness and depth of your stare
leave me asking how and why?
It's like the creator took a piece of the night sky
and placed it in your eyes.

And these windows to your spirit are
more powerful than the sun and the stars.
Far from being a mere manifestation of creation,
I want to worship you for the Goddess that you are.

So bless me with your presence
every day and every night,
ignite creativity with your touch
like the horizon receives from sunlight.
Y me siento feliz cada vez
que veo tu sonrisa hermosa
and the light in your eyes
can make an estrella selosa.
Por eso,
te adoro como una diosa preciosa.

With skin the texture of silk
and color of earth,
your worth
can only be explained by saying
your mother blessed us with your birth.

Indeed,
everything about you communicates strength & power
beyond comprehension,
not to mention
that your natural radiance always grabs my attention.
Whether rocking trenzas
or with your hair pulled back –
black like your ancestors passed down to you –
you're proud of that fact.

Y tus palabras?
Llegan con las nubes,
dándome la esperanza para seguir.
Como la lluvia que cae sobre la tierra,
me ayudan crecer,
me ayudan vivir.

Porque en toda honestidad,

there's no doubt,
that a veces
me siento como planta
in times of drought.
'Cause when we're apart,
I start to miss
the pure bliss
that accompanies the tender moisture of your kiss –
your luscious lips against mine,
our
minds, bodies, and spirits divinely intertwined.

And for these reasons,
I want to provide you with flower and song
for so long,
you would think it was your wedding and funeral
gone the furthest from wrong

In fact,
I want to shower you with so many beautiful words
that their power
keeps you refreshed for more than just a few hours.

Porque tu eres "'in xochitl"
y yo "in cuicatl"
creando armonía
cada día
con poesía.

So I wrote this poem for you.
But like a letter
that's been returned to sender,
no llegó a su destino.
Sino
es el mío que busco en este camino.

And for now on this path
alone
as you
walk
your own.
I await the point when our paths converge,
surge con nuestras energias as they begin to merge
into one -
side by side
with balance,
power,
and pride.

But until that fateful day,
I leave you this poem,
recipient nameless
and unknown.

If Was a Tortilla by Ara Cruz

Minute Mensos would point to my shape
as evidence that brown people are illegal aliens
from another planet.
Granted es un circulo sagrado
but they see a UFO,
an invasion,
and the ability to plan it.

Some "Americans" would want to keep me,
well,
a bleached white version at least
because they want our food,
culture,
and labor to feed the beast
but not mi gente,
not me

If I was a tortilla,
some people would still mispronounce my name
claim it was tor-tila
with little to no shame.
Or worse,
like Jose to Joe and Maria to Mary
scary how they could Wrap me
as my cultural identity they bury.

If I was a tortilla,
other people might try to convince you to replace me,
saying that I am not good enough for you,
that,
why don't you use a fork or a spoon.
But you would not listen to those haters

because you and me are tight.
In fact,
our relationship was pre-arranged.
Far before we met,
our destinies were set.
It is in your DNA
to hold me the way you do.
See,
like your ancestors,
you eat with me
and I feed you.

If I was a tortilla,
they might find and burn all my people
equal to what the Spanish did to Native codices
see this would be the sequel
as they develop elaborate plans
on stolen lands
to hunt down mujeres
who with their hands
imprint in me
la fuerza de nuestros antepasados
sagrado es la forma
que me han dado.

But you might be asking,
"Why would some people do such a thing?"

Because if I was a tortilla,
I would represent evidence
of Brown people's residence
on this continent
long before the present tense.
In fact,
with me as proof,

"illegal alien" and "immigrant"
would be the farthest from the truth.
'Cause I'm like the codices
see,
they would have to get rid of me.

How else could they deny the facts
that of an Indigenous people
with immense knowledge
that remains intact?

Even though Mayan stories of creation
may be hard for some to believe,
see,
there is no denying the fact
that I would be made from maiz,
corn
harvested
with the genius of our ancestors
and the primary food for most Native people
for so long,
the only thing we need to point to
to show that we belong.

Born and raised in Denver, Ara Cruz is a Xicano/Indigenous (Nahua/Genizaro Tiwa) spoken word artist, educator, and organizer who finds himself standing on the shoulders of those women and men who have struggled to maintain traditions and dignity. With this strong sense of responsibility, he tries to walk in a good way every day in order to better his community. Graduating from the University of Colorado at Boulder with a B.A. in Ethnic Studies (emphasis in Chicana/o and American Indian Studies), he now works with youth in

Denver as an educator, advocate, and workshop presenter. Using the experience he gained in campus and community organizing through MEChA (Movimiento Estudiantil Chican@ de Aztlan), Oyate (Native student group), and other organizations, Ara became a co-founder of Café Cultura and now serves Executive Director. Knowing his talents are a gift from Ometeotl, the Creator, he has shared his flor y canto (flower and song) with people of all ages. Through his poetry, he attempts to place a smoking mirror in front of his people and society in general, in an effort to make all of us think, speak, and act in positive ways.

Beautiful Struggle by Fabiola Flores

I come from a place
where people lift up gang signs
instead of a warm hand to shake.
But there is always beauty
in the struggles other people face.
I come from a place
where respect is only received
by those who have lighter skin
and my skin color
should be something supposedly
to be ashamed of.
But I find being brown
as being blessed.
I come from a place
white people call home,
where I was labeled
as an "Abandoned Child"
or just another student
who will get pregnant in a while.
Because I am brown,
people confuse me for dirt.
For the people who say that,
thank you.
Dirt is a part of nature!
You use products
to change who you are.
But I am born with natural beauty.
Others have an easier path
while I have to build my own tracks.
I would like to be labeled as a survivor,
instead of an abandoned child.
I would like to meet that man society calls a father.

But then I pull back
because I need to spend time with the man
who has stepped up to fill that role.
The people who have never had a chance
to taste a simple struggle
will never realize the beauty
that once was created from it.

―――――――――――――――――

Fabiola Flores is a Sophomore at DSST College View.

The Real Me by Marilyn Yobech

I am the Palauan girl
who no one ever talks about,
someone that is a blur in everyone's eyes.
But I am here to make myself clear,
make myself known.
I am a girl,
not just ordinary.
I am a Palauan girl from a long line of creative people.
I am come from a beautiful place
where the waters are crystal blue,
not murky and polluted by trash.
I come from a place
where we can unite
instead of driving a wedge between us.
We do not have pizza
and chicken
but we do have tama,
crunchy on the outside
but soft
and chewy on the inside,
like our people.
We have hard shells
but once you get to the inside,
the soft sweet side is revealed.

My father was a person so great,
yet left my life.
In so doing,
he made me stronger,
showing me the real world.
I am the phoenix
that rises from the ashes.

I rise up from the pain
and suffering.

―――――――――――

Marilyn Yobech is a Sophomore at DSST College View.

www.ingramcontent.com/pod-product-compliance
Lightning Source LLC
Chambersburg PA
CBHW071147090426
42736CB00012B/2262